BRIAN WILSON IN SWANSEA BUS STATION

BRIAN WILSON IN SWANSEA BUS STATION

Poems

Graham Fulton

RED SQUIRREL PRESS

First published in the UK in 2015 by Red Squirrel Press
www.redsquirrelpress.com

Red Squirrel Press is distributed by Central Books Ltd.
and represented by Inpress Ltd.
www.inpressbooks.co.uk

Designed and typeset by Gerry Cambridge
www.gerrycambridge.com

A CIP catalogue record is available from the British Library.

ISBN: 978 1 910437 09 4

Printed in the UK by Martins the Printers Ltd. on
acid-free paper sourced from mills with the FSC chain
of custody certification.
www.martins-the-printers.com

Contents

Stance 3

For my wife Helen, and Brian Wilson

Stance 1

Brian Wilson in Swansea Bus Station

Immaculately groomed
        and cunningly disguised
as a Welsh bus driver
                        Brian Wilson
                        of the Beach Boys
        stands beneath the canopy
of Swansea bus station
        in search of
                        the normal life
                he can never have
with a badge on his jacket
        and a song in his heart
as he waits for the X15
                        to pull in
                        while the rain
        buckets down on the roof
and takes his place at the wheel
        and pulls out
                        as gracefully as
                a Malibu surfer
riding the waves
        and splashes up the hill
to God Only Knows where
                        while whistling
                        'Wouldn't it be Nice'
        from the classic album
Pet Sounds
        with a rabbit-caught-
                        in-the-headlights
                look on his face
as the passengers sing the chorus
        menacingly in tune
if this was

a parallel universe
which it

is

Lord of the Flies in Hampton Court Palace

Dead
Nobel Prize-
             winning author
                    William Golding
is dressed as a Tudor peasant
and leaning groggily
                    against a wall
             in the Clock Court
and pretending to be on the verge
of vomiting
                    while inwardly considering
             the duality of man
and the chaotic savagery
of our basic nature
                    as a daytrip tribe
             of Goldingesque schoolboys
in red jumpers and grey shorts
leap on his back
                    and kick his shins
             and thump his chin
and strangle his neck
while screaming KILL HIM KILL HIM
                    and taking no notice
             of the female teacher who shouts
and shouts and shouts
and
shouts
                          and all that's missing
             is the organic facepaint
and the pig's head on a dystopian stick
                    and a democratic shell
full of water   sand
and a little blackhaired boy called Simon

                    or a little blondhaired boy
                 if you prefer the movie
         being cradled allegorically out
         to sea

The Holy Goalie Saves Our Souls
10/7/1998

On the roof of West Kennet chambered tomb
David Icke   goalie and shaman
dances around a Grandstand blaster
                yodels along with a B.C. cassette

His singing is pish   but very sincere
He means every dissonant
                stone age note

His beardies are grooving about as well
                His women
are shuffling around their beads
the way that they did with handbag piles
before *The Keeper* enlightened the path
                explained the offside rule in the dark
trying their best not to look like twats

It's too late for that
        but never the world

The guru's mantra
                enters the tomb
and lances the boil of preconception
totters the Champions League of truths
That's the nut from the BBC …
the wanker who said that Arran would sink!

Perhaps it did on a day still to come
There's so much that we don't understand
        When to attack and when to defend
and who is the bastard in the black
        The way the Universe raced to its end

He holds his balls
                    but can't hold a tune
The planet's a safer place with loons

Alan McCready's Brief History of Slavery

With Tom Sawyer on the back seat
and a smiling monkey dangling from his mirror
Alan skilfully negotiates
the ranks of multi-coloured cars
            in the multi-storey town centre car park
and happily tells me
                yesterday he saw
a white polythene bag puffed up with air
    caught in the branches of a tree
                        while immediately behind it
a black polythene bag also caught in the branches
        was inflating then deflating
inflating   deflating
with a poly-erotic rhythmic pulse
            and flapping against the one in front
    which made him think of slavery
or some bizarre inversion of slavery
    as we happily steer
through time   space
                in this infinite man-made car park
and tells me I would certainly
have written something about it
        if I'd really been there to see it
which is never going to happen

Sorley MacLean at Renfrew Unemployed Workers' Centre

27/2/1987

for Jim Ferguson

He asked if we preferred doing it
standing up or sitting down

We both replied *Standing up*

He then stood
gave a mythical reading in Gaelic
full of Skye   storms   soil
       music   water   humanity
empty of vanity   pettiness
        envy   judgement
all the darkness that kills us
with his eyes closed
      Our eyes open
       The way I remember
to an audience of seven
including Jim   myself
We didn't understand a word
knew exactly what he meant

He left on the arm of a happy woman
He's gone

I'll never forget   be sure
if he was asking
about life or death

John McGarrigle in The Clutha

29/11/2013

something to do with
                    the grace of chance
a shatter of thoughts
                              rhythm of heart
             the randomness
of being a life

        a fellow
traveller

something to do with
                  darkness falling
down through the dark
                              leaves from the trees
                 at the end of November
a favourite table
            nursing a beer
tapping to Ska
                thinking of poems
                      you've left behind
       and truths you've yet
to tell
     with flowers and bees
                      and a junkie
            climbing through the window
to steal your TV
                      a real world
          a helicopter dropping
onto the roof
          a mad story
     no one would ever
believe

the randomness is
          too cruel
it's almost as if
          it's been perfectly planned

it hasn't
          it's just the way
of finding yourself in this space
          this time
our human situation
          at the mercy
of ourselves
          living until you're
no longer living

Glasgow's McGarrigle

there's something waiting
          for all of us
each moment
       this moment
is a last

          grasp your moments
dance

Greyfriars Bobby Spins in His Grave
G8 Summit   Edinburgh 6/7/2005

A silver balloon in the shape of an 8
        ascends towards
    the porridge-grey sky
Thirty forensic policemen and women
        take it in turns to glare and say
Can you stand back please
     I've told you before
to a pair of drugstuffed Burke & Hares
       who blunder about the Academy steps

A bongo slapper walks the line
     of starship troopers with visors   shields
       The Parliament keep is ringed with wire
a monkeysuit minstrel plays air guitar
     A posse of sweaty testosterone sheriffs
pound up the Mound to capture a lass
       who's armed with a locked and loaded can
of Scrumpy Jack   a tea cosy hat
     Americans snap the rioting teams
       resume their quest for haggis and malt

      The Little Mermaid is kicked to hell
dyslexic colours all over the mud
     Thumbelina is ripped apart
flowers of Scotland all over the rock
       A common or garden insurgent who's got
a MOCK UN helmet insists that *They have*
     more freedom in China
than we do here
      William Wallace grins on his spike
the Parliament door is singed by fire

Anarchists scan their wrong-way-up maps
to find where Greyfriars Bobby sits
on top of his plinth   a silent growl
Mary Queen of's head grows back
The Banks of Alba are whistled to bits

The Dog that was Tied to the Railings

at the foot of the steps
outside the offices
         everyone

     comes to ask for answers
  concerning
houses falling
   around our heads
roofs blowing off   chimneys collapsing
wallpaper peeling away   too slowly
for the naked eye to comprehend
        it barks
it barks   it barks
    it barks   a barking nova
of breedless angst
stares

at the closed door
          ignores
       the floral display
     empty Ribena carton
constellation of fag ends
         water dispenser
vacuum cleaner
it barks   it barks   it barks
it barks
the railings

  climbing the edge of the steps
     the answer
every one   falling

The Warrior Race on Bath Street

first a girl on
  a boy's back
     out
   of their heads
  laughing glass
smashing five or six
piling in
with fists boots charging
up the hill not seeing
   the shoppers
    hiding
against the walls of
banks lawyers bistros
the zenith
of civilisation
     letting them
    steam past booting
      roaring throwing
   each other to
the road stamping
one face
as it melts in the centre
     the vortex
    people
   silent behind
their two-way mirror watching
a primal fury
take shape letting
them get on with it

The Scream at ASDA

a woman screaming into
                 the face of a man
on the other side of
                 the superstore window
with glass so thick
                 no sound can be heard
                 not caring who sees as

she screams
         marches away
looks over
         her shoulder to see
if he's watching   returns   screams
                 marches away
looks over her shoulder
                 to see if he's watching
returns   screams
         without a sound   not caring
             who sees as

her mouth makes
         the shape of BASTARD
         her eyes never leaving his
his eyes never leaving hers

The Last King of Glasgow
13/9/2006

for the Kelvingrove Tyrannosaurus

A musty Mesozoic display
decades beyond its dump-by-date
Ex-T. Rex! Lizard King!
The Kelvingrove One
                  is now extinct

He reckoned he had a job for life
ruling the *Creatures From the Past*
They've bumped him off
                wheeled him out
He's gone to the tar pit in the sky

It's just as well   the CGI kids
would laugh and point
                piss their pants
when they saw his wobbly Sixties teeth
spindly arms   bandy legs
a softy from a plasticine age

Farewell my misproportioned friend
who *ROARED* above me
              taught me to dream
Museum piece! Magnificent chump!

We couldn't keep up with HD bones
          21st Century spoon-fed thrills
There's no room left
for worlds of our own

The Destruction, by Fire, of the School of Art Library

23/5/2014

Black smouldering
cremated wet front page lumps
instead of
an intimate enchanted glade
Dreamscape lamps on long chains
like mini skyscrapers
forged from folded holed metal
with pink   blue
simple exotic glass
and strong slender tree trunks
stretching into
a handmade Scottish heaven
A cool secret forest
of books   wood
knowledge   grace
a living room that seems to
be hanging in space

                        a space

of seamless silence
of desks   paper   curves   time
fingerprints   breath   ghosts
a tender unpretentious beauty
created from nothing
returned to nothing
The dark balcony set back
and the tall Glasgow windows
welcoming in the same lost light

Sissy Spacek in *Starbucks*

In a pink padded jacket
        sprinkled with
ban-the-bomb symbols
           the Sissy Spacek lookalike
   who looks nothing like Sissy Spacek
crunches down hard
on her first lollipop of the day
       and reads a few more lines
     from *Carrie* by Stephen King
       in between
staring sociopathically
at the slowly moving queue of adults
      including a woman
    with purple streaks in her hair
who could possibly
be her mum

         as if by the sheer force
of her telekinetic pre-pubescent will
      she can make the whole
grown-up coffee shop
begin to shake
     and the roof collapse
in a gorgeous apocalypse
of plaster and paint
     and the light bulbs explode
   and the glass case
full of croissants and baguettes and
cookies   pastries   plastic bottles
of mineral spring water for
a reasonable price disappear
     into nothingness forever for
a little while at least

David Attenborough's Life of Elastic

With a comforting Darwinian voice
             and a pair of baggy shorts
        natural-born-naturalist
David Attenborough
enters Paisley
      with a huge budget
      bulging in his pocket
and a camera crew hot on his heels
           to try and find out
        the significance of all
the red elastic bands
that have started appearing
        on pavements and stairways
      and why sometimes
two are found close together
as if they are trying to mate
      and if they have a social conscience
    or are they the end of evolution
and why people keep on disappearing
           on their way to the post office
        and if we'll all eventually
turn into red elastic bands
when we fall asleep
      like something from
      Invasion of the Body Snatchers
           because David knows
          reason and logic don't always
keep the world from falling apart
as he takes a photo of a gorilla
         from his dinosaur-skin wallet
      and whispers into the camera
They're already here   You're next

Charles Darwin in *Sainsbury's* Toilet

'Man on the Moon' by R.E.M.
is coming out of
the speaker in *Sainsbury's* toilet
as I assume the position
in an alarmingly pristine cubicle
with comfortingly giant amounts of
planet-friendly flushable roll   it

really is eardrum-bouncing loud
and the quality of sound is exceptional
I can pinpoint
every bass line
and every epic deep south sweep of guitar
and every word old baldy in his glittery make-up
is singing about Newton
and apples
and Darwin and Elvis   and once

the survival-of-the-shittest deed is done
I'm standing washing my hands in front of
the sign that commands me to wash my hands
and the giant mirror
with my shoe tapping
and my eyes crossing
and wondering what the hell it all means
as he warbles on about Mott the Hoople and St. Peter
and the game of life   I suppose

it's about not having faith
in the information we're fed by the ones
who concoct the official history
of us
gravity

or heaven
or nothing   but

I still like to convince myself
the decision to wash my hands is entirely mine

Nelson Mandela in the Bank of Scotland

In a manic depressive suit and tie
        instead of his trademark
flowery psychedelic shirt
        Nelson Mandela
ex-convict and friend to the rock stars
        enters the Bank of Scotland in Swansea
looking much younger
        than he does in real life
        with slightly less white hair
and a spring in his step
        as he strides up to
the smiling girl at the counter
        with every intention of saying
        "Where the fuck has my money gone?"
being careful not to put his hands across
        the 'Do not put your hands across this line' line
in case the shutters slam up
        and gas starts to pour out
        from craftily concealed nozzles
and the baton wielding credit limit police
        or the global recession execution vans
or the anti-icon death squads
        pull up outside and pump him full
        of soft-headed bullets
without giving any warning
        because this is the land
of Oliver Cromwell and Clement Attlee
        Charles Hawtrey and Bernard Bresslaw
        Carry On Up the Khyber
and the Black and White Minstrel Show
        and the Morriston Orpheus Male Voice Choir
singing 'Free Nelson Mandela'
        in their *Free Nelson Mandela* T-shirts

and we have every right
to know why we are
being kept apart from our life savings
as we have our heads blown off

Andy Murray Loses the US Open Final
8/9/2008

Leaning on the window sill   watching the silence
orange streetlamps   wet pavements   parked cars
no one there   not even a wino
serenading the midnight rain

most of the houses are switched off   a few still alive
doing the same thing I am   leaning   listening
to the radio
          disembodied voices
talking about advantage   love   the importance
of being Scottish   the breaking point of parked cars
streetlamps   disembodied transmissions
               the distance
the signal is still to travel

a fox nipping across the grass
among the whirlies   between the wheelies

it's not dark enough for the stars to come out
dark enough for silence   a backhand volley
the distance travelled from nowhere to Scotland
stars exploding   applause   light

Stance 2

The Murder of John Lennon
by Roman Polanski

In the never-sleeping City of Life
>> people queue up to photograph the spot
where an *ex-Beatle* was shot
on a Monday night
>> and seem disappointed there's no chalk outline
>>> of a body on the sidewalk
>> or a loudspeaker endlessly playing
>>>> 'Give Peace a Chance'
and squint up at the windows
to catch a glimpse
> ofYoko peeping between the curtains
>>> or Rosemary's Baby shaking a rattle
>>> or Roman Polanski
> in a false Charles Manson beard
or only the ghost
of Boris Karloff
>>> who walks the laundry
in his Universal boots and Jack Pierce make-up
yearning for the days of burning windmills
>>>>> tidy endings

but I could have told you Boris
Monsters don't always look
the way you'd Imagine
>> and if you close your eyes you can almost see
Chapman assuming an assassin stance
> and Mia Farrow in a mini-skirt
and the late great John Cassavetes
>> who died after an operation
for cirrhosis of the liver
>>> which happens sometimes

                              apparently
                and the Smith and Wesson
        singing its happy *White* album song
             as his Lennon specs flew into the air
        and he reached for the dark

The Discovery of America

The door of our cleaner's cupboard
on the seventh floor of our three star hotel
at 7th Avenue 56th Street
        is lying open
                she's nowhere around

I peek inside to see
it's well-stocked with plastic bottles
full of lotion   soap
shampoo and toilet rolls
in greenly soothing crinkly wrappers
which makes me think
            of virgin forests
on unexplored continents
       water dripping from giant leaves
and scantily-clad natives
        ripe for exploitation
in my cynical
Christopher Columbus mind
          as well as
bin liners   shower caps
sprays and squirts

      and placed among them
        the heart of everything
her crucifix
some writing in Spanish
     a cereal packet prince and princess
     a photograph of two old movie stars
in a heart-shaped frame
      and a picture of a saint
with a halo around her miraculous head
which in this moment

           is quietly touching

                     important

a humble shrine for the human being

sanitary products

an enviable faith in heaven and hell

New York Doggy Style

Four-legged fiends come tearing out
of their exclusive apartments
at the speed of light
                    and piddle politely
in all the proper places
                    as professional dogminders
try to control their misfit packs
of Poodles   Shih Tzus   Pomeranians
        Bichon Frises   Llasa Apsos
                    a Chihuahua called Miguel
        and other balls of fluff
they haven't thought of
a name for yet

            and here comes one now
being pushed across the road in a baby's buggy
and one with a pink tutu
and one with its head sticking out of a bag
and one with blue suede shoes
to protect its paws from the scorching concrete
                    and last but not least
a micro-terror wearing Raybans
        leaning out of its macho-master's mega-blasting
gas-guzzling I-rule-the-world monster roller's window
                    and yapping patriotically
        in an American accent
which accurately translates as
YOU TALKIN' TO ME?
or I'M BARKIN' HERE!
    or GET SOME GET SOME! at anyone
whose face doesn't make the grade
which is everyone

The Dawn of Man in the Chelsea Hotel

With infamous green slacks
> and an Aleister Crowley hairstyle
>> the doorman/bouncer of the Chelsea Hotel
tells us it's safe to come inside
as long as we don't stray any further
than the lobby
> which is occupied by three people
tapping away
at their deviant laptops

> and that's okay by us
as we have no desire
> to climb the stairs
> and knock on the door of room 100
where Sid killed Nancy so they say
while singing 'My Way' in a white tuxedo
or the room
> where Arthur C. Clarke
> wrote *2001: A Space Odyssey*
> while disguised as an ape
the room
> where Dylan Thomas
> stumbled about with a bottle of whisky
> while reciting the very long name
of a Welsh railway station
the room
> where Jack Kerouac
used his *On The Road* roll of paper
> to wipe his bottom by mistake
the room
> where Arthur Miller
> wrote *The Crucible*
> while disguised as Marilyn Monroe

or the room
          where William Burroughs
      had his lunch of Andy Warhol Campbell's Soup
            while fully clothed
or something like that
                  and we're quite content
to stand here and think of
Dylan   Sid   the black monolith from *2001*
and Arthur C. Clarke disguised as Arthur C. Clarke
                  as they dance along the corridors
                        in a big conga line
and all the other phantoms on the floors above us
shaving their armpits in the infamous bathrooms

Joe Turkel

something *has* to be written

about the wee guys
we take for granted

about the wee guy with froggy eyes
who was Lloyd
the smiling bartender beyond death
with a gantry of ghostly alcohol
in *The Shining*
directed by Stanley Kubrick
and said things like
Your credit's fine Mister Torrance
as he poured Jack Nicholson
another Jack Daniel's

and Private Arnaud
in *Paths of Glory*
where he was shot at dawn
by a French Hollywood firing squad
directed by Stanley Kubrick
and Tiny
in *The Killing*
directed by Stanley Kubrick
where he was riddled near the end
after saying a couple of words
no one
can hear

dying forever   over
and over   looped
in celluloid amber

and Tyrell   the god of The Replicants
in *Blade Runner*   who had his
chess-playing eyeballs squidged out
by Rutger Hauer's thumbs
who I've also not seen
for a long time   he might be
dead
or making adverts
or both

flickers of immortality
digitally remastered

an unsung loser
a presence at the edge

reborn forever
like a foetus in space

Rock-Ola

these redly sparkly plasticky booths
to fit an unclear family
in Lori's nuclear family diner
love
replica America   huge replica car sprayed
with paranoia cobwebs   hubcaps   fins
fenders   trunk   brain on the back seat
lifer waitresses
in perky hats   ankle socks
Asian girls   hung pictures
of James Dean before his crash
John F Kennedy   ketchup   syrup
      boy wonders
                        best of all
the intimate tabletop jukebox
        slot the quarters
flip the lists   wait
for the flying saucer-size plate
of pancakes   ham
hash browns   Beach Boys
soul   surf   sit
with shoes tapping
brain bobbing   miming
every last word   listening
for my replica
Brian Wilson missile crisis belly
to explode   Otis   Marvin
Chubby Checker   cooked Americans
surf the soul
love   death   sunny
side up

Between One End of the World and Another

Staring into the eyes of a bobcat puppet
in a Californian gift shop   a price
round its neck   too real
glass
        looking inside
                the white lines
at Tom Waits growling
Joni Mitchell soaring   white lines
on the freeway   staring
into windows   cars
Pacific licence plates
        a long line from home

These lives are smoke   fires on the hills
hot   burning   hair on the arms
a Joshua tree reaching for heaven
a shredded tyre like snakeskin
           girls   boys   playing I-spy
looking for the exit
            talking to themselves

turbine blades   a farm of wind
why do some move
        and others remain
staring

into the eyes of a dog
half-way out of a pick-up's window   too real
for words   why do some move
others remain   still?
Something

        beginning with d

dinosaurs behind a drive-thru
life-size

Mark Rothko at the Tate Modern

On the wooden benches in front of
                    Untitled
grown-ups get lost in the subconscious paint
blacks in blacks   suicidal maroons

interpret the canvas   the wall around it
never let go of their audio guides
                keep their comfortable lives at a distance
see what they want in the nameless oil

Right up close
a bouncing critic   red-haired
possibly   five years old
gives her opinion   points   shouts
                Pinky! Pinky! Pinky! Pinky!
                Pinky! Pinky! Pinky! Pinky!

Colour holds no terror for her
Emotional depths just make her laugh

The Tarot Cards that Ginsberg Touched

In Baader-Meinhof black
    and armed with
a shaggy black beard
                Allen Ginsberg
            invaded Europe
        sometime in the Seventies
as all the hairy kids
        sat on the floor
                gaping in awe at
                    his shaggy black poems
and swaying about with
        their hairy mushroom eyes
and Timothy Leary ears
                    and you asked him
            back to your house
        and gave him cold beer
to make his head spin
        and hot pizza to fill
                his streamofconsciousness tummy
                and the chance
to not have to be
        a howl-performing monkey
for just a little while
                before the next gig
            in West Berlin
        or Berwick-upon-Tweed
as he played karma poker
        with your bumper pack
                of Dalai Lama tarot cards
                and left his hairy DNA
all over the magician
        and the sorceress
and the fool

and death and cheese
in his transcendental beard

now it's d	ark my head swelling with jet lag	bursting
with jet la	g standing for a glimpse of the m	adman
from Mont	ana with his shirt buttoned up to	the neck
his sprig of	lucky white heather in his top p	ocket
and no tie o	f something smart to say such a	s *My teeth*
are bleeding	or *Now it's dark* or *You're nex*	t *fucker* or *Life*
is full of sur	prises to the neck and no tie or	Life is full
of heaven in	the blackness with my maharis	hi pen
in the Glasg	ow Film Theatre darkness they	won't let me
in without a	ticket my Dennis Hopper head	all swelling
with transatl	antic jet lag he's here all smiles	and inner peace
as the fires r	age across the dry canyons of L	os Angeles
and wearing	his skinny tie and black coat aft	er all and
signing book	s to say such as My teeth are in	the dark
with his wav	y grey hair *can you sign this fo*	r *me please David*
please and *Th*	*anks very much David* which i	s all I can think to
look straight i	n to my Mulholland eyes or str	aight into his to
think of all the	darkness to which he replies *Y*	*ou bet*
with a smile bu	rsting up my earthbound head	bledding

Die Michael Palin, Die

I bullet into Glasgow on the no-seats train
    to get his autograph for my girlfriend
because maybe she'll like me a bit more

    but he's already
        high
on the unconquered second floor
among the poetry and philosophy
    and all the psychology doorstops
nobody in their right mind ever visits
    with his snug blue jeans
and housewives' choice smile
        as he sits
            and scribbles his way through
an Everest of copies
        of his latest bestseller
        and excites the ladies of all ages
who are queuing down the stairs
            across the first floor
        down
to the ground
as they hug their holy grail tickets
        which only go up to 300
because after that you're a no one

    and I'm 301 because I came too late
and he's up above me
    with his happiness and royalties
and wife and children and respect
    and contentment and beguilingly-
Pythonesque-Lewis Carroll-Oxbridge-
    footlights-punting-along-the-river-
with-a-lumberjack-shirted-yak-milking-

tradition of loveable English quirkiness
        and next time I'll bring a gun
and empty it into the back of his head
        or push the heaving racks of Leonard
and Catullus and Milton and Pickard
        and Rimbaud and Reznikoff and Poe
down on top of him or smudge him to death
        with my copy of *Catcher in the Rye*
as I whisper *Die Michael Palin, die*

The Death of the Painter Steven Campbell
16/8/2007

I met him   once
He asked me to come and read
in Kippen community hall

He hired two girls   one black one white
to pose in the nude for local kids
with nothing to be   choices to make
        Do it today or not at all
Do your best or fall through space
Poems   paint   whatever works
                Quixote in the Pictish fog
losing his balance   weary grace

Artlessly barmy   frontier hair
making him look like
Wild Bill Hickok   slinging ideas
An old man child

I said my lines in absolute dark
except for a torch he held at my face
giving me just enough to see
the naked models circling round
changing direction   white
then black   Sense him
at my right   left
hunting around me   tilting against
the bland   safe   spinning   burning
flaring   fasterchanging
gone

Someone Said *Joe Strummer is Dead*
22/12/2002

Joe Strummer had Dickensian teeth
and a white riot voice
and wasn't too hot at fancy guitar
                     I preferred
the goasfastasyoucanness of The Damned
the artfuldodgerness of The Pistols
the blackhairness of The Banshees
the leatherjacketness of The Ramones
to the Clash's
three minute manifestos

but the tears begin to burn
when someone tells me he
is dead

his wife in the kitchen
roast potatoes in the oven

and I'm travelling on hands and knees
among the legs and the sweat
in a lost world of bouncing crowds
as The Adverts sing 'Gary Gilmore's Eyes'
        and Fay Fife of The Rezillos
is saying *Excuse me pet*
as she tries to get past me
to the stage of the Silver Thread
which isn't a stage at all
and Siouxsie is wearing thigh length boots
and Poly Styrene is wearing a brace
        and Dave Vanian is singing
Is she really going out with him?
with a voice that doesn't fit his face

and The Buzzcocks are trilling happily
about orgasms and *Boredom*
    and Joe is growling *What's My Name?*
like an IRA bomb about to explode
as he shows us who we are

and two boys are sniffing glue
in a dark corner of a disco
with a Golden Wonder packet
like something out of hell
as teenage pints go sloshing across
the dancefloor
    and someone is pulling the plug
from my neck as we faithfully sing
God Save the Queen
at the tops of our voices
without knowing or caring or falling
apart   caring too much

and I'm giving breath
to all those gone friends
                  I can still find
in the time and space in my head
who were wasted in the brain
as they crawled along the pavement
in the chemical Central Belt rain
    who were killed by out-of-control cars
driven by thirteen year old thieves
    who joined the police
or became swimming instructors
   as we pogoed off the edge of the Earth
laughing at you   laughing at us

and falling through somewhere
we didn't want a name for
                           raging into
the crippled normal sub-zero night
with our safety pins and dog collars
and grinning role model Sid Vicious zips
and bondage trousers electric shock hair
and padlocks on chains round our throats
and my life in the oven
as I still feel this blood ignite
                make something real
with the only chord we can play

My Baby Played Me *searching for the young soul rebels* by Dexy's Midnight Runners Which was Given Away Free with the *Daily Mail*

I had been reading Sylvia Plath
It really cheered me up

I Like Albert Einstein

There's this site among the billions of sites
which features the wisdom
of the mad-haired kind-eyed
mad-kind German-Jewish nutter
and genial genius
with his tongue sticking out of his mouth
and relativity pouring out of
his massive kind-mad brain
laid out
over
24 or more virtual pages
with a long list of cool quotes on each one

and he's wittering on
about science and god and women and men
and logic and illogic
and it's all very moving and profound
but as you travel
from page 1 to page 2 and page 2 to page 3
and page 3 to page 4
then the number of computerised people
who say *I like this*
with a big enthusiastic thumbs up
begins to implode rapidly

in fact
it shrinks from about 16,000 people
rabidly liking the quotes on page 1
to about 1 person quite liking the quotes on page 24
as people get a bit bored
with all the mad-haired philosophy and click
on to something else a lot more black hole-ish
and thoughtless

and void of equations
and it's such a lot like the unhinged bubble we
find ourselves in expanding away getting colder and
further and silent and further and everything until there's
nowhere left to go

Come Oan Keira

Come oan Keira   come oan Keira
                    will you

        will you
                    move it
will   you   just   move it Keira
move it Keira
Keira
        KEIRA
                    whit ur you dayn Keira?
come oan Keira   COME   OAN   KEIRA
            will you move it will you
move yur fuckin arse Keira
come oan Keira come oan Keira
                            whit ur
            whit ur you

whit ur you dayn?
WHIT UR YOU DAYN KEIRA?
                    COME OAN KEIRA
                    COME OAN KEIRA
MOVE IT KEIRA MOVE IT KEIRA
KEIRA   KEIRA   RIGHT
            THAT'S IT
am goin now
bye Keira   bye Keira
am away now
        am away now
                        am goin
            am gone
bye Keira
am away now Keira
Keira   KEIRA

WILL   YOU   JUST
MOVE IT KEIRA   av goat ti
git up the road

Swimming to Ireland

On the bus into town
the clock on the News Channel
suspended from the ceiling
is frozen at 11.17

39 minutes behind when we are

The giant red words
SEAMUS HEANEY'S FUNERAL
fill the bottom half of the screen
Petrified poets fill up the top

Millionaires   presidents
rock star messiahs
Terrorists who have seen the light!

On the seat behind me
a wee girl says to her daddy
Daddy   that wee boy over there is a bad boy
he was shouting at his mummy
                    That's right sweetheart
            I'll kick your bum
            if you shout at your mum
Can we go to that pub daddy
and get a drink? I'll have a Coca-Cola
                I don't think so sweetheart
Does grandad live in that house daddy?
                    No sweetheart   he lives in Ireland
            We'll be going to see him soon
Will we swim there?
                    No sweetheart
                    we'll ride in a big boat

It's all
unmiraculous
It's all "drumming your fingers
on the kitchen sink"

Nothing that needs
enshrined on the page

The digital flatscreen spasms to life
The numbers click on

We drip towards heaven in our own truth
Reach for the causeways
we've shaped in our minds

Stance 3

The Anarchists on the Eight Sixteen

One   two
                    a herd of chaos
        bumping   barging   out of a field
on to the road with wobbling udders
        yellow numbers attached
to their ears   the cars

                            wait
at the makeshift lights
                    look straight ahead
at the 816   Lochgilphead road
windscreen wipers
bovine cabaret   couldn't care less
drovers prodding them on their rumps
                    hoofing about
on the dung-slapped tar
                            The bull

who rules
this rudderless gang
                is hugely humping
            his cow of choice
    keeps falling off   getting back on
                            The men
at red
look straight ahead   oblivious to
our horny king
            still trying to hump
his cow of choice
keeps falling off   getting back on

Dr. Manhattan's Fluorescent Blue Penis

As we watch *Watchmen*
              in our edge-of-town multiplex
        the woman on the seat in front
suddenly leans forward
              vomits onto
        the nicely sticky plastic floor
        at precisely the same moment
Mothman is carted off to the asylum
              which prompts the person to her left
        to move a few seats further to the left
        as her husband or partner
on this journey through life
puts his arm around her shoulder
    guides her tenderly into
    the cheap Tuesday darkness
                    never to be seen again
in this edge-of-civilisation oasis of culture
              with its fading 1951 version
of *The Day the Earth Stood Still* poster
                    its rustling bags
of existential popcorn

                    and we forget all about her
keep on watching
with increasing euphoria
    Dr. Manhattan's timetravelling
atomic blue tadger
        a man dressed as an owl
as they save us all from self-destruction
whether we want it or not

The Great Paisley Boxing Day Earthquake

I'm suddenly waking in 1979
The headboard of my bed is battering
against my bedroom wall for thirty seconds
                        more or less
                until it stops
and it's suddenly   quiet

I'm out of bed and onto the landing
Everyone else is doing the same
We're all laughing   knowing it's
an earthquake which
                        doesn't happen
                in Scotland
for heaven's sake

It was gloriously feeble
compared to the ones they have
                in Chile   or Haiti
which kill thousands
    of people in the blink of
an eye

but it's Our earthquake

In the morning all we find
is a wine glass that's been
                        sliced in half
which I keep as a souvenir
In 1992 I discover it in a cupboard
                        and throw it into
                the dustbin
without a second thought
One of those old metal bins

                    with a lid
            that didn't quite
fit

I can see it now
A work of genius
fragile and dazzling
amongst the eggshells and peelings   The future
                    is a dislocation
          The present
a silent echo

The Autopsy of Jah Wobble

I told you I dreamt I had
woken from a dream
and told you that Jah Wobble
from the first incarnation
of Public Image Limited
had died
with his black hat

I went looking for a copy
of their second album *Metal Box*
to put on a turntable as a tribute
but on the way
I heard a loud electrical sawing noise
and through a pane of glass in a door
I saw an autopsy being carried out
with two men
with their white sleeves rolled up
to find out how he died   an arm
was already off   the still-attached stump
a perfect meaty circle   I turned away
and continued to look
and through a second door
I saw him propped up on his right arm
in a white bed in a white room
with his face removed
below the eyes
a perfect meaty oval   Later
I opened
my usual tabloid
frantically scanned the pages
to see if there was any mention

of Jah Wobble the bass guitarist
of Public Image Limited rhythmically expiring
on the previous day but there wasn't

The Love Dance of N. Kaplinsky

27/1/2005

BBC teeth   Breakfast TV
Natasha is reading the autocue script

Auschwitz-Birkenau   sixty years on
The sound is down   the stereo's up

We play *Public Image* while munching our bran
John Lydon is wailing inside our brain

I picture Himmler's farmyard face
Mengele children   tattooed ghosts

It's all too much at seven a.m.
We need some easy   meaningless   un

demanding   vacuum   skin
and gloss   Narcotic Kaplinsky   BBC hair

We could be wrong we could be right
We dance to *Rise* while rinsing our bowl

It does not mean we have ceased to care
but LIFE is exploding inside our soul

Grangemouth Twinned with Mordor

to the right of the train
is a delightful refinery
which looks a bit like somewhere
from *The Lord of the Rings*
with its
chimneys   pipes
and impressively nauseous metal structures
and cooling towers
and white tubercular clouds slouching above it
and a flare of angry flame
that seems to come from a hole in a hill
which looks just like an Olympic flame   possibly
an Olympic flame
for the Mordor Olympics
                              currently taking place
with only one ring on the flag   including
Trolls playing bowls with Hobbits' heads
and Gollum attempting to leap the crack of doom
with a sponsor's logo on his loincloth
and the terrible Dark Lord falling eye-first
into the water jump of the steeplechase
with the Orcs sniggering behind
their claws
                    until
it occurs to me that probably
my time would be more meaningfully spent
contemplating the massacres in Syria in 2013
or the massacres in Pakistan in 2014
or why I've just moved my hand from this space
to this space
or why someone has just had

their dad's ashes turned into a tattoo on their arm
or what keeps everything being everything
so I'm going to stop right now

David Carradine's Wardrobe of Choice
3/6/2009

Discarding his enlightened pyjamas
        and Tarantino sunglasses
      softly-spoken spiritual role model
David Carradine
      enters the wardrobe
         of his hotel room in Bangkok
     to have some quality
auto-erotic time to himself
         because a life
of theological contemplation
      has taught him
         that what really counts
is starving your brain of oxygen
     for a few lonely seconds of genital pleasure
         before slipping gently over
              to the other side
    with a Narnia-like
         expression of divinity on your face
      as if it never really mattered
about knowledge   meaning
         hate   love
or what you'll be remembered for
         or leaving a tip for the cleaner
         or what a bozo you're going to look like
when she finds your body in the morning
     because David knows
         that when we cease to exist
then so does the world

Suranne Jones in Royal Exchange Square

With yellow hair
    and a serious beanie
        sexy ex-
Coronation Street siren
Suranne Jones
        is walking between
    the Gallery of Modern Art
and the empty shell of *Borders* bookshop
with a Blackberry in her right hand
    and a map of Glasgow
        in her left hand
      and straight past me
  in the general direction
of Buchanan Street
      and I say to myself
    'That was Suranne Jones'
  followed by *'but Suranne Jones*
has dark hair'
    before heading on my way
  in the specific direction
of who knows where
    with a final look
as she disappears

      and three days later
I find in the paper
she's in Glasgow
    playing a serious role
      a picture of her
with dyed blond locks
      and I try to wonder
        what would have happened
if I'd continued down Buchanan Street

                     instead of turning left
or if *Borders* had still been selling books
                          or if I'd bought the *Daily Mail*
          instead of the *Daily Record*
or if my mum and dad
          had never been born
or if no one was ugly
or if no one was beautiful
               or if our ancestors had never struggled
out of the sea and onto the land

The Garden of Earthly Delights by Hieronymus Bosch

Glasgow Green hosted a daily entertainment 'Live Zone'
during the 2014 Commonwealth Games

Callum

stoap playin in thi dirt
    an come an huv
yir photie taken!
      snaps a mother to her son
who seems reluctant
to go anywhere near
    the topiary manifestation
of the evil grinning thistle-man *Clyde*
       who's presiding over
   this sordid orgy
including
Bonnie Prince Charlie on stilts
      an incubus dressed as a seagull
dark breathing tents selling
shots nachos blasters fajitas
prime venison hog roast
    proud lines of foul-smelling chemical boxes
totie children racing a virtual Usain Bolt
but never winning
as green-for-go paramedics shoulder their way through
past ice cream drug vans
shaded security friskers
hedonistic hot dog cabins shivering mobile clouds
of bugs-bunny-dinosaur-one-eyed-
monster balloons
     sharks on strings
       a red plastic dragon's wing
trampled in a smush of mud

below a creepily   slowly   revolving wheel
with lost horizons
           all the way to Hampden Park
                              the planets beyond
                    next to
star-fried super-studs with traffic cone hats
quantum mechanical shacks
black bacchanalian portals promising
cold happiness   onions   hot merchandise
a human
triumphantly scraping something
brown from a bowl
a poetry reading behind a Gent's urinal
                         as a woman says
         fuckin shut it to her son
who's crying because
he's just dropped his candy floss
                         as if saying
         fuckin shut it to her son
will make the towering hedge-faced mascot god
of the 2014 Commonwealth Games
and all his malevolently pleasant minions
                    sink back into the sphincter of hell
from whence they sprang

Usain Bolt in Glasgow
1/8/2014

as the zenith
of evolutionary perfection
grabs his baton
and legs it down the lane

a gap-eyed up-to-date ghost
unconscious
of someone who's
actually achieved something
with their life

sits beside her mum
on her sixty quid seat
and posts some vacuous chatter
on her twatter app

The Man who Liked to Talk in the Cab

nay problum pal
Christ will yi look ut thi state uh that
ah canny staun drunk wimmin staggerin aboot
thi streets thurz nay dignity ah yewsti like
a drink masel but thur ur too many bampots
in thi world so ah jist huv wan ur two an
then ah go hame
how lang
huv yi been married ah wiz married
fur twenty year
ah met ma wife in thi Savoy its
funny how thingz work oot if
ah hudni gaun inti thi Savoy that night
weed niviruv met
an weed niviruv goat divorced
but at least ma kids still talk ti me an
ma grandkids still talk ti me so ah must
be dayin somethin right ha ha yi jist huvti
git on wi thingz yi just huvti
bounce back thurz nuthin else fur it
sheez livin
wi ur sisters noo
talk aboot thi two ugly sisters mair like thi three
ugly sisters ha ha when ah went ti thi lawyer he wuntit ti
charge me wan hunnert an twenty five pound an hour
fur Christ sake ah telt him whur ti go
so whiddyi day
poetry ah canny staun aw that Robert Burns stuff
ah canny be bothirt wi aw that langwij ah prefer
ti spen ma spare time fishin thi rivers ah saw
somethin thi other night aboot lighthooses
an they wur aw built by Robert Looee Stevenson
ur sumdy relaytit tay im

ah widni mind gon ti live in a lighthoose
ah suppose yi jist huvti git on wi thingz
yi jist huvti bounce back ah suppose thatull
be twenty wan pound please cheers pal see yi later

Shakin' Stevens is Not Dead

Huv a look ut this son!
Susan Boyle's new Christmas ellpee!

it sez on thi back thi first song iz
'Oh Come All Ye Faithful'
which she duz wi Elvis Presley

that canni be right

ah thought Elvis wiz deid

he died sittin on thi bog
so how kin she be singin a jewett
unless sheez got some conneckshun
ti thi hereaftir

a wurd in god's ear

ah suppose they got an old recordin
an put er alangside im
singin
joyful an triumphant
wi aw that tecknickul stuff they kin
day theez days

they kin day anythin!
they kin huv er singin wi sumdy
sheez nivir met
whooz singin somewhere else
on thi other side uv thi world

maybe she kin day mair jewetts
wi deid folk like Bing Crosby
ur Shakin Stevens ur John Lennon

they kid day Imajin!

it wid be really nice
ecksept he goes on aboot
thur bein no such place uz hevvun
so it widni be very Christmassy
wid it?

Christmas withoot hevvun
jist widni work

Christmas withoot Susan Boyle
jist widni work

The Bin Lorry on Queen Street
22/12/2014

Reverse the machine
                          rewind the film
the image burned
                    within your mind

imagine

        the scattered unwrapped presents
the tinsel   the tags
flying back into
                the bags for life
the blood reflowing
                   into the veins
the dead returning
                onto their feet
resuming their smiles
                futures   fates
the casual chatter
           a hole of chaos
a way in

        a refrain

to explain
        you'll never wake
in the morning
           and know in a flash
that this is the day
            a Council lorry
will mount the pavement
               ride its line
all the way to

                    the station
    the end

                past

green men
            red men
restaurants
            shelters
statues of
            the great long gone
the solstice fun fair
                        in the rain
the unfair funfair
                    laughing bodies
useless rhymes
                and helpless loves
a rhapsody
            unable to catch
the pain of now
                        us
as time slows
                up
                    speeds
down

and two days later
                I walk
the same route
                the monster took
look

over my shoulder
to see if it's there
                    the wheels
the tyres
        the headlamps like eyes
lift

a red plastic turtle
                    from the edge
at the lights at
                    the George Square crossing
a survivor with
                    a missing flipper
a favour from
                    a split cracker
a way out

        a gift
from nowhere

The Statue on Paisley Cenotaph

Facing south
        high on the stone
                above the wreaths
above the kids
on their skateboards

a Scottish king on his grey horse

cast in iron
helmet and visor
pennant streaming

and four Great War soldiers

two on each flank
protecting him
as he protects them

with heads bowed
helmets and ponchos
always wearily
trudging forwards

a declaration
of tradition and death

the tradition of death
in someone else's land

Flodden   Ypres
Helmand Province

dignity for sanity's sake

forged in bone
cast in iron
always staying
in the same place

above the kids
and their Big Macs
high on the stone
                    above the future
                            Facing south

Robert Tannahill's Underpants

With a swashbuckling coat
and a feeling of inadequacy
                    Robert Tannahill
        weaver of garments and weaver of verse
jumps into the water in 1810
                and proceeds to drown
among the shopping trolleys
and thrownaway computers
            in a place that will always
be known as Tannahill's Hole in Paisley
                after no one bothered to publish
his second slim volume
                            which is a real shame
as he came out with some good stuff
                    including words like
            bonnie and *lassie*
but *no one*
is allowed to interfere with
            the omnipotence
                of Robert Burns The King
who made a smart career move
                by dying young
            after a colourful spree
of rural excess and poetic fornication
                        and I'm looking
into Tannahill's Hole right now
with its graffitied culvert
including good stuff such as RAB-M
            WULLY   MAXI YOUNG BOYS
and a big grey pair of stripey underpants
draped over a rock
            which might have been worn
                by Robert on that fateful day
but probably wasn't

E-mail Attachment Containing the Exact Second the Life of Tommy Cooper Comes to an End

PLAY he's in front of a curtain
                    left arm outstretched
while wearing a black suit and white shirt
bow tie   fez
        at four seconds his blonde female assistant
            in a wispy purple outfit
enters the view
and helps him put on a shiny gold magician's coat
        he says *Thank You Love* at nine seconds
            at fourteen seconds a change comes over
his face   he touches the assistant
on her small right shoulder with his huge left hand
and quickly crumples to the floor
                    he's facing the camera
        the smiling assistant
lifts away the microphone stand
in preparation for the next trick
                        his eyes are closed
        he's making peaceful breathing sounds
from twenty two seconds until thirty three seconds
        he's tilting backwards as a belching noise
comes out of his mouth   his fez doesn't fall off
his arms and legs are moving   slowly   almost
gracefully   and the audience are laughing
their heads off STOP

I'm Lazarus ... Get Me Out of Here

We can watch *Celebrity Dump*
from the comfort of our flatline minds
         and watch *Celebrity Facelift Gone Wrong*
and watch *Celebrity Facedrop Gone Right*
             watch *Celebrity Exit*
as original thinkers   long ignored
arrive to expire
on Snuffcam Prime

watch *Celebrity Stomach Pump*
watch *Celebrity Shooting Up*
watch *Celebrity Necrophile*
watch *Celebrity Paedophile*

and watch *Celebrity Resurrection*
Elvis   Michael   Adolf and Jesus
trumpet fanfares   torn from time

watch *Celebrity Hump*
as the golden couple of the day
do sex in a new contortion of love
as long as they're caught on Camera One
     and watch *Big Orwell's Placenta!*
as we vote for the latest accessory wean
named Krakow   Caracas or Ulan Bator
depending on where
the foetus was sold   the loser
neatly   deleted off screen

I'd Like to Thank Bela Lugosi

for saying *Listen to them   children of the night*
as he stood on his cobwebby steps
while undead armadillos
scuttled among the coffins and droppings

and Lon Chaney for wearing a forty pound hump
and dying of cancer in time for the talkies

and Dwight Frye for swallowing flies
and Dwight Frye for dying in poverty
while trying to feed his family
and William Henry Pratt for being Boris Karloff
and Boris Karloff for saying *We belong dead*
after getting a knockback from his girl

and Elsa Lanchester for hissing like a snake
and Conrad Veidt for somnambulating
across impossible Weimar rooftops
with black rings under his eyes
and Max Schreck for having a baldy head
and John Barrymore for having a pointy head
and King Kong for tickling Fay Wray's tum
as her dress conveniently fell apart

and Lon Chaney junior
for having a hairy terrier face
as he stalked the dry-ice woods
in his workie shirt and baggy breeks

and Claude Rains for whacking him on the napper
with a silver-tipped cane and who can blame him
and Boris Karloff for saying *Goood!*
and Boris Karloff for saying *Friend?*

and good old Bela for saying *To die*
to be really dead   that must be   glorious

for being buried in his cape
for showing us there is more than being in colour
for showing us it's perfectly fine from behind the sofa
THE END is nowhere to be afraid of

In the Time I've Spent Waiting for the Bus to Gallowhill

I could have watched the last five minutes of *Jaws*
four times or read 'Rhapsody on a Windy Night'
by T. S. Eliot eight times or played one and a bit sides
of *Pet Sounds* including the time
it takes to turn the record   or watched
the shower scene from *Psycho* twenty seven times
or had sex sixty times or looked at five paintings
by Vincent Van Gogh for four minutes each or
four paintings by Francis Bacon
for five minutes each   or drunk one
or possibly two gin and tonics or peeled one hundred
and twenty one bananas or played *Northern Sky*
by Nick Drake five and a third times or stood at
the window and watched the cars crashing into
the lamp post at two in the morning once   or sharpened
sixty pencils   or wandered aimlessly
in WH Smith twice or eaten eight Cadbury's Twirls
at a leisurely pace or been in control of my destiny once
or watched the last ten minutes
of the final episode of season five of
Buffy the Vampire Slayer twice   or flown one third
of the way to Swansea or walked one two hundred
and thirty nine thousandth of the way to the moon
or thrown myself in front of a moving train
one thousand two hundred times   or thought of
all the long gone wasted time and all the wasted time
yet to come once or watered two hundred and forty plants
instead of standing here waiting for the number 20 bus
which is now 21 minutes and 20 seconds late

Acknowledgments

Some of these poems have appeared before in the
following publications:

*Chapman, 60/60 (Daemon 7 &8), Ambit, Gutter,
Poetry Cemetery* (USA), *The Eildon Tree, Lyric,
Word Riot* (USA), *Barbaric Yawp* (USA), *Staple, Fire,
Other Poetry, Viral Cat* (USA), St. Mungo's Mirrorball
Website, *Hidden City Quarterly* (USA), *Painted, spoken,*
Southbank Centre Poetry Library Website, *Poetalk* (USA),
The Potomac (USA), *Poetry Super Highway* (USA),
Northwords Now, San Pedro River Review (USA),
*Causeway/Cabhsair, Southlight, Orizont Literar
Contemporan* (Romania)

Graham Fulton's eight critically acclaimed books of
poetry include *Knights of the Lower Floors* (Polygon,
1994), *Full Scottish Breakfast* (Red Squirrel Press, 2011),
One Day in the Life of Jimmy Denisovich (Smokestack Books,
2014), and *Photographing Ghosts* (Roncadora Press, 2014).
He's also published over 15 pamphlet collections, and is
co-author of *Pub Dogs of Glasgow* (Freight Books, 2014). He
was a contributor to the anthology of translated
Palestinian poetry *A Bird is Not a Stone* which was
published by Freight Books in 2014. He runs Controlled
Explosion Press and lives in Paisley.